This journal belongs to:

Gaby,

I hope you enjoy keeping record of your marriage as years go by. I

D1295686

a .

Wedding Day
12.9.15.

How Do I Love Thee?

How Do I Love Thee?

A Devotional Journal for Wives

Jennifer Flanders

PRESCOTT PUBLISHING
Tyler, Texas

Scripture references marked NASB are taken from THE NEW AMERICAN STANDARD BIBLE ®, Copyright ©1960, 1962, 1963, 1968, 1971, 1972, 1973, 1975, 1977, 1995 by the Lockman Foundation. Used by permission.

Scripture references marked NIV are taken from THE HOLY BIBLE, NEW INTERNATIONAL VERSION ®. Copyright ©1973, 1978, 1984 by International Bible Society.

Scripture references marked ESV are taken from THE HOLY BIBLE, ENGLISH STANDARD VERSION ®. Copyright © 2001 by Crossway Bibles, a publishing ministry of Good News Publishers.

Scripture references marked GWT are taken from GOD'S WORD® TRANSLATION of THE HOLY BIBLE, © 1995 by God's Word to the Nations. Used by permission of Baker Publishing Group.

Scripture references marked NLT are taken from THE HOLY BIBLE, NEW LIVING TRANSLATION, ©1996, 2004. Used by permission of Tyndale House Publishers, Inc. Wheaton, IL 60189. All rights reserved.

Scripture references marked NKJV are taken from THE HOLY BIBLE, NEW KING JAMES VERSION, ©1982, by Thomas Nelson, Inc.

Scripture references marked KJV are taken from the authorized version of THE KING JAMES HOLY BIBLE.

Scripture references marked YLT are taken from YOUNG'S LITERAL TRANSLATION. 1898, by Robert Young. Public Domain.

Scripture references marked NET are taken from the NET (NEW ENGLISH TRANSLATION) BIBLE, ©1996-2006, by Biblical Studies Press, L.L.C. http://netbible.com. Used with permission. All rights reserved.

HOW DO I LOVE THEE: A DEVOTIONAL JOURNAL FOR WIVES
Copyright ©2015 by Jennifer Flanders. www.flandersfamily.info

The vast majority of clip art in this book is from a set of 9 CDs my husband bought me back in 1996 called *Masterclips 101,000 Premium Images Collection*. This was long before I started blogging or writing or publishing *anything*, and I hadn't the foggiest idea what I'd ever do with such a thing — but I held onto it, just in case, and now I use it all the time! Additional clip art was procured through a premium membership to The Graphics Fairy, *http://thegraphicsfairy.com/*

All rights reserved. No part of this book may be used or reproduced in any manner whatsoever without written permission except in the case of brief quotations embodied in critical articles and reviews. For information, please address Prescott Publishing, 3726 Woods Blvd, Tyler, TX 75707. http://prescottpublishing.org

ISBN: 9781938945151
LCCN: 2015950138

Dedication

For my daughters & daughters-in-law:
With a prayer that God will bless your marriage
with as much love and joy and happiness
as He's lavished on mine.

Contents

INTRODUCTION

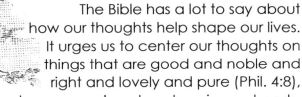

The Bible has a lot to say about how our thoughts help shape our lives. It urges us to center our thoughts on things that are good and noble and right and lovely and pure (Phil. 4:8), for out of the treasure we've stored up in our hearts, we will speak (Luke 6:45). If our hearts are full of good things, good things will flow from them. If not, not.

That's why it's important that we, as wives, cultivate an attitude of gratitude and learn to focus on our husband's most positive, admirable, and endearing qualities. Our marriages cannot help but benefit when we discipline ourselves to do this.

That's the purpose of this journal in a nutshell. The pages and prompts are designed to help you recall and record all those things you love most about your husband, to reflect on your most cherished memories, and to recognize God's hand at work in your relationship. Since the happiest marriages are those founded upon the Truth of Scripture, you'll also find lots of Bible verses scattered throughout these pages. I pray your marriage will be blessed as you meditate on God's Word and apply it to your life.

May His richest blessings be yours,

Jennifer Flanders

How Do I Love Thee?
(Sonnet 43)

by Elizabeth Barrett Browning

How do I love thee? Let me count the ways.

I love thee to the depth and breadth and height

My soul can reach, when feeling out of sight

For the ends of being and ideal grace.

I love thee to the level of every day's

Most quiet need, by sun and candle-light.

I love thee freely, as men strive for right.

I love thee purely, as they turn from praise.

I love thee with the passion put to use

In my old griefs, and with my childhood's faith.

I love thee with a love I seemed to lose

With my lost saints. I love thee with the breath,

Smiles, tears, of all my life; and, if God choose,

I shall but love thee better after death.

God's Plan
for
Marriage

"So God created mankind in His own image, in the image of God He created them; male and female He created them."

- Genesis 1:27, NIV

It is not good for the man to be Alone. I will make a Helper suitable for Him.

- Genesis 2:18, NASB

Side by side & hand in hand:

"For if either of them falls, the one will lift up his companion.
But woe to the one who falls when there is not another to lift him up."

- Ecclesiastes 4:10

God's purpose for marriage:

Mathew 19:4-6

Ephesians 5:24-33

1 Corinthians 7:2-9

Malachi 2:15

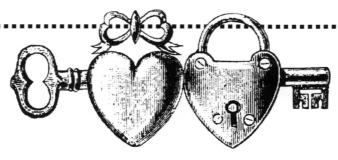

Marriage is to be a reflection
of Christ's relationship to the church.

"This mystery is great; but I am speaking
with reference to Christ and the church."

- Ephesians 5:32, NASB

How can I more accurately reflect Christ's love in my own marriage?

"In your relationships with one another,
have the same mindset as Christ Jesus."

- Philippians 2:5, NIV

God designed marriage...

"Have you not read that He who created them
from the beginning made them male and female, and said,
'For this reason a man shall leave his father and mother
and be joined to his wife, and the two shall become one flesh'?"

- Matthew 19:4-5, NASB

...for our benefit and His glory.

"Let us rejoice and be glad
and give him glory! For the wedding
of the Lamb has come, and
his bride has made herself ready."

- Revelation 19:7, NASB

"Take my yoke upon you and learn from me, for I am gentle
and humble in heart, and you will find rest for your souls.."

- Matthew 11:29, NAS

Life before
Marriage

My Childhood

"When I was a child, I spoke and thought and reasoned as a child. But when I grew up, I put away childish things."

- 1 Corinthians 13:11, NLT

My Schooling

"Study to show yourself approved unto God, a workman that needs not to be ashamed, rightly dividing the word of truth."

- 2 Timothy 2:15, KJV

What I was doing when I met my husband:

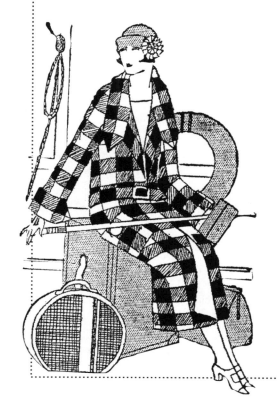

"Remember the former things long past,
For I am God, and there is no other;
I am God, and there is no one like Me."

- Isaiah 46:9, NASB

What he was doing when he met me:

"Remember the days of old; consider the generations long past. Ask your father and he will tell you, your elders, and they will explain to you."

- Deuteronomy 32:7, NIV

My Friends

"Oil and perfume make the heart glad,
and the sweetness of a friend comes from his earnest counsel."
- Proverbs 27:9, ESV

His Friends

"A friend is always loyal,
and a brother is born to help in time of need."

- Proverbs 17:17, NLT

How we met:

"Praise the LORD, the God of Israel,
who has sent you to meet me today!"

- 1 Samuel 25:32

First impressions:

"Receive him then in the Lord with all joy,
and hold men like him in high regard."

- Philippians 2:29

When I knew _____ I was smitten...

"Many waters cannot quench love; rivers cannot sweep it away."

- Song of Solomon 8:7, NIV

How love bloomed:

"There are three things that are too amazing for me,
four that I do not understand: the way of an eagle in the sky, the way
of a serpent on a rock, the way of a ship in the middle of the sea,
and the way of a man with a maid."

- Proverbs 30:18-19, NASB

Dear Diary...

Our
Courtship

Our First Date

"… record this date, this very date…."

- Ezekiel 24:2, NIV

All the Details

How he asked me out: _____
_____
_____

Where we went: _____
_____
_____

How long we stayed: _____
_____
_____

What we wore: _____
_____
_____

Who else was there: _____
_____
_____

What I thought: _____
_____
_____

How long he waited before asking me for a second date: _____
_____
_____

Our Growing
Friendship

AS IRON SHARPENS IRON, SO A FRIEND SHARPENS A FRIEND.

- Proverbs 27:17, NLT

What most attracted
me to my husband:

What most attracted
my husband to me:

How we spent time together:

There is "a time to weep and a time to laugh;
a time to mourn and a time to dance."

- Ecclesiastes 3:4, NASB

There is a time for everything,
and a season for every activity
under the heavens.

- Ecclesiastes 3:1, NIV

Favorite Activities

"So I recommend having fun, because there is nothing better for people in this world than to eat, drink, and enjoy life. That way they will experience some happiness along with all the hard work God gives them under the sun."

- Ecclesiastes 8:15, NLT

Favorite Hangouts

"The whole earth is filled with awe at your wonders;
where morning dawns, where evening fades, you call forth songs of joy."

- Psalm 65:8, NIV

"And I will betroth you to me forever. I will betroth you to me
in righteousness and in justice, in steadfast love and in mercy."

- Hosea 2:19, ESV

Our Engagement

THE RING

"I adorned you with jewelry: I put bracelets on your arms and a necklace around your neck, and I put a ring on your nose, earrings on your ears and a beautiful crown on your head."

- Ezekiel 16:11-12

The Proposal

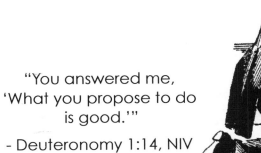

"You answered me,
'What you propose to do
is good.'"

- Deuteronomy 1:14, NIV

Reactions of family and friends:

"So you too should be glad and rejoice with me."

- Philippians 2:18, NIV

Premarital books and counseling we received:

"Plans fail for lack of counsel, but with many advisers they succeed."
- Proverbs 15:22, NIV

*Please Join Us
for a
Bridal Shower*

Wedding Showers

"Every good thing given and every perfect gift is from above,
coming down from the Father of lights,
with whom there is no variation or shifting shadow."

- James 1:17, NASB

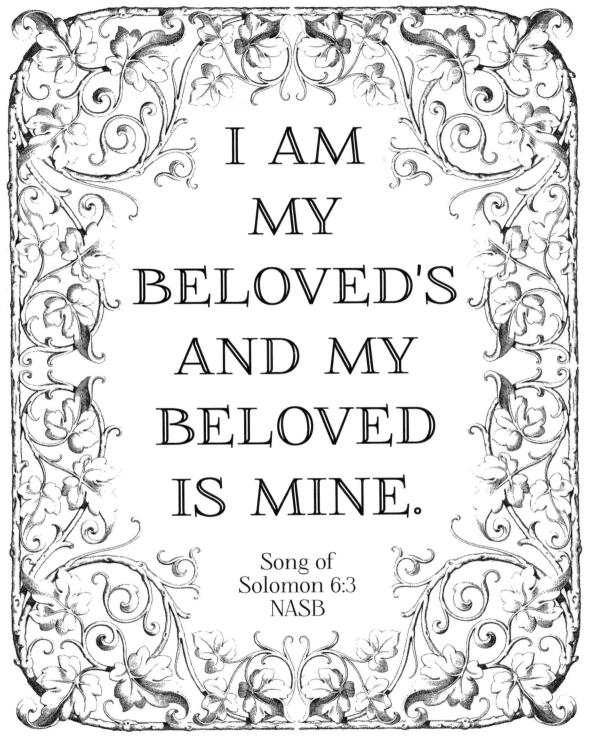

I AM
MY
BELOVED'S
AND MY
BELOVED
IS MINE.

Song of
Solomon 6:3
NASB

Making Plans

"The mind of man plans his way, but the LORD directs his steps."
- Proverbs 16:9, NASB

Invitations

"... both Jesus and His disciples were invited to the wedding."

- John 2:2, NASB

The Wedding Dress

"The bride, a princess,
looks glorious in her golden gown."

- Psalm 45:13, NLT

The Bridesmaids' Dresses

"You cannot make the attendants of the bridegroom fast
while the bridegroom is with them, can you?"

- Luke 5:34, NASB

The Rehearsal

"Rehearse among nations His glory,
Among all the peoples His wonders."

1 Chronicles 16:24, YLT

The Rehearsal Dinner

"At the time of the banquet
he sent his servant to tell those
who had been invited, 'Come, for
everything is now ready.'"

- Luke 14:17, NIV

"Let us hold fast the confession of our hope without wavering,
for He who promised is faithful."

- Hebrews 10:23, NASB

Our
Wedding

Our Wedding Ceremony

"I will fulfill my vows to the LORD in the presence of all his people."
- Psalm 116:18, NIV

Our Wedding Vows

"It is better not to make a vow than to make one and not fulfill it."

- Ecclesiastes 5:5, NIV

The Wedding Venue

"I was glad when they said to me,
'Let us go to the house of the LORD.'"

- Psalm 122:1, NASB

For better or worse
For richer or poorer
In sickness
and in health
For as long as we both
shall live

Our
Wedding Music

"Let us come before him with thanksgiving
and extol him with music and song."

- Psalm 95:2, NIV

Our *Photographer*

"Then those who feared the LORD spoke to one another, and the LORD gave attention and heard it, and a book of remembrance was written before Him for those who fear the LORD and who esteem His name."

- Malachi 3:16, NASB

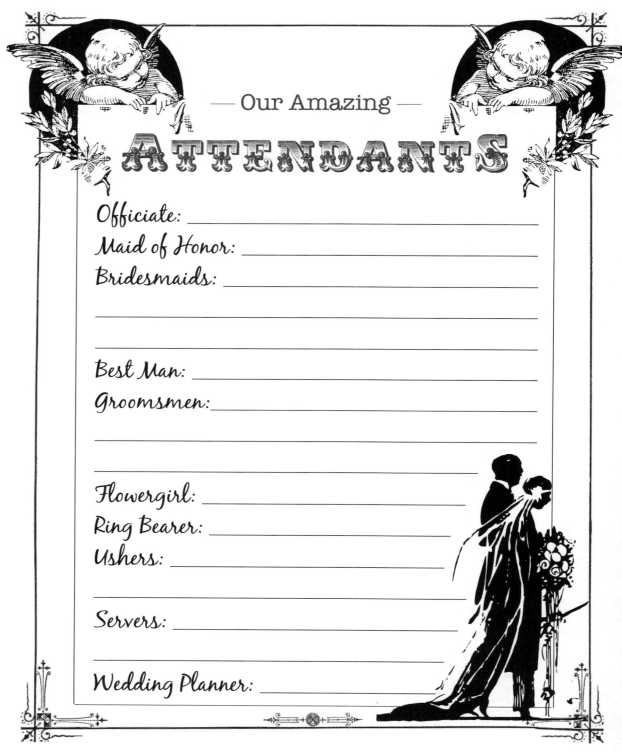

Our Amazing
ATTENDANTS

Officiate: _____

Maid of Honor: _____

Bridesmaids: _____

_____

_____

Best Man: _____

Groomsmen: _____

_____

_____

Flowergirl: _____

Ring Bearer: _____

Ushers: _____

_____

Servers: _____

_____

Wedding Planner: _____

THIS CERTIFICATE OF

MARRIAGE

Certifies that

_____ of _____

and _____ of _____

WERE BY ME UNITED IN

HOLY MATRIMONY,

at _____ in the State of _____ in accordance with the Laws of the State of _____ on this _____ day of _____ A.D. 20 _____

In Presence of _____

Signed _____

The Reception

"Receive one another, then, just as
Christ also received you, to God's glory."

- Romans 15:7, NET

Dinner and Dancing

"The young women will dance for joy,
and the men--old and young—
will join in the celebration."

- Jeremiah 31:13, NLT

o not urge me to leave you or turn back from following you; for where you go, I will go, and where you lodge, I will lodge. Your people shall be my people...

& your God my God.
Where you die,
I will die, and there
I will be buried.
Thus may the
Lord do to me,
and worse,
if anything but death
parts you and me.

Ruth 1:16-17, NASB

Going Away

"So they left by boat for a quiet place, where they could be alone."

- Mark 6:32, NLT

Our
Honeymoon

The Send Off

"Why didn't you tell me,
so I could send you away
with joy and singing
to the music of timbrels
and harps?."

- Genesis 31:27, NIV

The Get-Away Car

"The wheels were made like chariot
wheels; the axles, rims, spokes and
hubs were all of cast metal."

- 1 Kings 7:33, NIV

going away

"I will go, but only if you go with me."

- Judges 4:8, NLT

How We Got There

A Night Afloat On A Wonder Boat!

"When they got there,
they found breakfast waiting for them...."

- John 21:9, NLT

Mr. and Mrs.

My New Name

"A good name is to be
more desired than great wealth,
Favor is better than silver and gold."

- Proverbs 22:1, NASB

My Trousseau

"And I will cause the Egyptians
to look favorably on you.
They will give you gifts when you go
so you will not leave empty-handed."

- Exodus 3:21, NLT

Our Wedding Night

"And the man and his wife were both naked
and were not ashamed."

- Genesis 2:25, NASB

Therefore,
what God has
joined together,
man must
never separate.

- Matthew 19:6, ISV -

"Marriage should be honored by all, and the marriage bed kept pure, for God will judge the adulterer and all the sexually immoral."

- Hebrews 13:4, NIV

The Early
Years

Goodbye, Old Life...

"I focus on this one thing: Forgetting the past
and looking forward to what lies ahead..."

- Philippians 3:13, NLT

...Hello, New!

"Therefore if anyone is in Christ, he is a new creature;
the old things passed away; behold, new things have come."

- 2 Corinthians 5:17, NASB

Leaving and Cleaving

"For this reason a man shall leave his father
and his mother, and be joined to his wife;
and they shall become one flesh."

- Genesis 2:24, NASB

LET THE WIFE SEE THAT SHE RESPECTS AND REVERENCES HER HUSBAND, THAT SHE NOTICES HIM, REGARDS HIM, HONORS HIM, PREFERS HIM, VENERATES AND ESTEEMS HIM; & THAT SHE DEFERS TO HIM, PRAISES HIM AND LOVES & ADMIRES HIM EXCEEDINGLY.

- Ephesians 5:33 -
(Amplified)

Our favorite way to start the day...

"My voice shalt Thou hear in the morning, O LORD;
in the morning will I direct my prayer unto Thee, and will look up."

- Psalm 5:3, KJV

...and our normal evening routine.

"When I remember You on my bed,
I meditate on You in the night watches."

- Psalm 63:6, NASB

Interesting Discoveries

"What has been is remote and exceedingly mysterious.
Who can discover it?"

- Ecclesiastes 7:24, NASB

New Adventures

"And I will give you a new heart, and I will put a new spirit in you.
I will take out your stony, stubborn heart
and give you a tender, responsive heart."

- Ezekiel 36:26, NLT

Our family's first car...

"You crown the year
with your bounty, and your carts
overflow with abundance."

- Psalm 65:11, NIV

... and the pleasure trips we took in it.

"[Wisdom] will guide you down delightful paths;
all her ways are satisfying."

- Proverbs 3:17, NLT

Special Outings and Date Nights

"Take me away with you—let us hurry!"

- Song of Solomon 1:4, NIV

LET EACH ONE OF YOU LOVE HIS WIFE AS HIMSELF; AND LET THE WIFE SEE THAT SHE RESPECTS HER HUSBAND.

Ephesians 5:33 ESV

J.L.T

"I thought about the former days, the years of long ago."

- Psalm 77:5, NIV

Setting Up
House

Our First Home

"…the builder of a house has greater honor than the house itself."
- Hebrews 3:3, NIV

THE WISE WOMAN BUILDS HER HOUSE, BUT THE FOOLISH TEARS IT DOWN WITH HER OWN HANDS.

PROVERBS 14:1

Moving In

"For in Him we live, and move, and have our being...."

- Acts 17:28

Getting Settled

"And you shall take possession of the land
and settle in it, for I have given the land to you
to possess it."

- Numbers 33:53, ESV

How we furnished our first place...

"By wisdom a house is built,
and by understanding it is established; and
by knowledge the rooms are filled
with all precious and pleasant riches."

- Proverbs 24:3-4, NASB

... and fixed it up inside and out.

"I undertook great projects: I built houses
for myself and planted vineyards."

- Ecclesiastes 2:4, NIV

Our Dream Home

"...make it your ambition to lead a quiet life
and attend to your own business and work with your hands."

- 1 Thessalonians 4:11, NASB

UNLESS THE LORD BUILDS THE HOUSE, THEY LABOR IN VAIN WHO BUILD IT.

Psalm 127:1, NASB

"Whatever house you enter, first say, 'Peace be to this house.'"

- Luke 10:5, NASB

Working Together

There's always lots of work to be done.

"There are six days when you may work,
but the seventh day is a day of sabbath rest."

- Leviticus 23:3, NIV

This is how we divide the chores.

"For we are co-workers in God's service; you are God's field, God's building"

- 1 Corinthians 3:9, NIV

Cooking

"She rises while it is yet night and provides food
for her household and portions for her maidens.."

- Proverbs 31:15, ESV

Cleaning

"She sets about her work vigorously;
her arms are strong for her tasks."

- Proverbs 31:17, NIV

Home Improvement Projects

"She watches over the affairs of her household
and does not eat the bread of idleness."

- Proverbs 31:27, NIV

Lawn & Garden

"She considers a field and buys it;
out of her earnings she plants a vineyard."

- Proverbs 31:16, NIV

Qualities of the Virtuous Woman

She is **RARE** and **VALUABLE**: *"A **capable**, **intelligent**, and **virtuous** woman—who is he who can find her? She is far more **precious** than jewels and her value is far above rubies or pearls."*

She's **TRUSTWORTHY, COMFORTING** and **ENCOURAGING**: *"The heart of her husband trusts in her confidently and relies on and believes in her securely, so that he has no lack of [**honest**] gain or need of [dishonest] spoil. She comforts, encourages, and does him only **good** as long as there is life within her."*

She's **HARDWORKING** and **INDUSTRIOUS**: *"She seeks out wool and flax and works with **willing** hands [to develop it]. She is like the merchant ships loaded with foodstuffs; she brings her household's food from a far [country]. She rises while it is yet night and gets [**spiritual**] food for her household and assigns her maids their tasks. She considers a [new] field before she buys or accepts it [expanding **prudent**ly and not courting neglect of her present duties by assuming other duties]; with her savings [of time and strength] she plants **fruitful** vines in her vineyard. She girds herself with strength [spiritual, mental, and physical fitness for her God-given task] and makes her arms **strong** and **firm**. She tastes and sees that her gain from work [with and for God] is good; her lamp goes not out, but it burns on continually through the night [of trouble, privation, or sorrow, warning away fear, doubt, and distrust]. She lays her hands to the spindle, and her hands hold the distaff."*

She is **GENEROUS** and **UNAFRAID**: *"She opens her hand to the poor, yes, she reaches out her filled hands to the needy [whether in body, mind, or spirit]. She fears not the snow for her family, for all her household are doubly clothed in scarlet."*

She is **CREATIVE** and **CONSCIENTIOUS**: *"She makes for herself coverlets, cushions, and rugs of tapestry. Her clothing is of linen, pure and fine, and of purple [such as that of which the clothing of the priests and the hallowed cloths of the temple were made]. Her husband is known in the [city's] gates, when he sits among the elders of the land. She makes fine linen garments and leads others to buy them; she delivers to the merchants girdles [or sashes that free one up for service]."*

She is **DIGNIFIED, JOYFUL, WISE**, and **KIND**: *"Strength and dignity are her clothing and her position is strong and secure; she rejoices over the future [the latter day or time to come, knowing that she and her family are in readiness for it]! She opens her mouth in **skillful** and **godly** Wisdom, and on her tongue is the law of kindness [giving counsel and instruction]. She looks well to how things go in her household, and the bread of idleness (gossip, discontent, and self-pity) she will not eat."*

She is **NOBLE** and is **LOVED** and **APPRECIATED**: *"Her children rise up and call her **blessed** (**happy, fortunate**, and to be envied); and her husband boasts of and praises her, [saying], 'Many daughters have done virtuously, nobly, and well [with the strength of character that is **steadfast** in goodness], but you excel them all.' Charm and grace are deceptive, and beauty is vain [because it is not lasting], but a woman who **reverent**ly and **worshipful**ly fears the Lord, she shall be **praised**! Give her of the fruit of her hands, and let her own works praise her in the gates [of the city]!"*

- Proverbs 31:10-31, AMP

How hard must my husband look to find these qualities in me?

```
J  O  Y  F  U  L  A  Y  H  T  R  O  W  T  S  U  R  T  P  U  B
M  U  P  R  A  I  S  E  D  I  D  C  D  U  M  R  A  N  O  M  L
T  Y  E  C  N  A  S  C  T  S  E  N  O  H  A  Y  E  E  D  L  E
R  D  S  A  K  I  N  D  N  T  R  I  O  M  A  M  N  E  W  R  S
Y  E  T  P  W  R  T  C  A  E  C  E  G  C  F  C  V  F  O  E  S
I  I  V  A  L  U  A  B  L  E  S  V  D  H  U  O  J  O  R  A  E
G  F  I  B  R  I  L  R  R  F  I  I  L  I  L  N  R  R  S  B  D
N  I  R  L  H  E  S  P  E  D  A  T  T  T  U  S  E  T  H  L  E
I  N  T  E  L  L  I  G  E  N  T  A  N  R  F  C  N  U  I  E  S
K  G  U  S  A  H  A  N  O  F  R  E  E  B  I  I  A  N  P  N  S
R  I  O  T  P  P  Y  B  D  R  D  R  R  I  A  E  L  A  F  C  G
O  D  U  E  P  T  L  I  S  U  Q  C  E  G  F  N  A  T  U  O  N
W  W  S  A  R  E  H  E  R  I  S  N  V  T  O  T  U  E  L  U  I
D  A  K  D  E  Y  D  P  M  I  T  E  O  R  I  T  N  N  R  F
R  L  E  F  C  L  I  N  A  F  V  O  R  W  S  O  I  D  S  A  R
A  H  T  A  I  G  A  W  G  U  E  F  L  I  T  U  R  I  Y  G  O
H  N  O  S  A  N  R  H  O  L  H  T  U  L  O  S  I  N  A  I  M
E  T  I  T  T  U  F  O  D  R  I  S  F  L  A  U  P  M  W  N  T
C  O  N  U  E  T  A  S  L  U  F  L  L  I  K  S  S  U  R  G  E
L  E  S  N  D  F  N  T  Y  P  P  A  H  N  Z  I  U  Q  D  I  L
G  E  N  E  R  O  U  S  E  M  X  I  T  G  N  O  R  T  S  O  F
```

(Solution on page 203)

"Let us not lose heart in doing good,
for in due time we will reap if we do not grow weary."

- Galatians 6:9, NASB

Two are better than One because they have a Good return for their Labor.

- ECCLESIASTES 4:9

"But on the judgment day, fire will reveal what kind of work
each builder has done. The fire will show if a person's work has any value."

- 1 Corinthians 3:13, NLT

Breaking
Bread

"... serve one another humbly in love."

- Galatians 5:13, NIV

What the Bible says about serving others:

My husband's favorite dishes:

"Prepare my favorite dish,
and bring it here for me to eat..."

Genesis 27:4, NLT

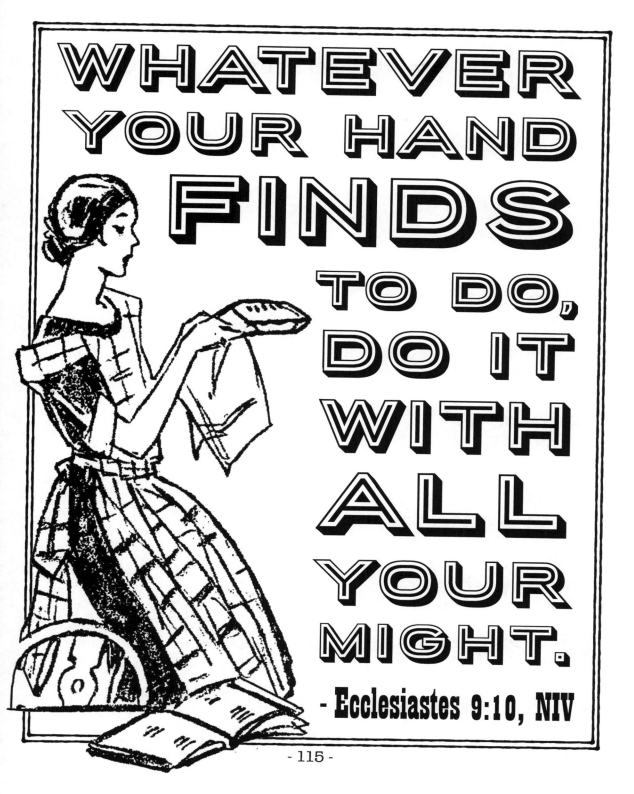

WHATEVER YOUR HAND FINDS TO DO, DO IT WITH ALL YOUR MIGHT.

- Ecclesiastes 9:10, NIV

Candlelight Dinners

"...the kingdom of God is not
eating and drinking,
but righteousness and peace
and joy in the Holy Spirit.."

- Romans 14:17, NASB

Our Favorite Restaurants

"Man ate of the bread of the angels;
[God] sent them food in abundance."

- Psalm 78:25, ESV

The Word of God is my sustenance.

""Man shall not live
on bread alone, but on
every word that comes
from the mouth of God."

- Matthew 4:4, NIV

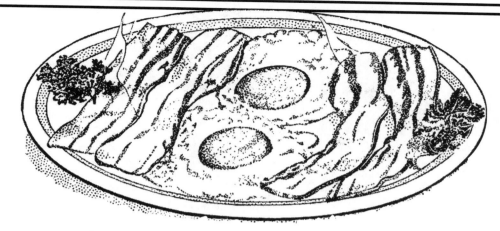

Whether, then, you eat or drink or whatever you do, do all to the glory of God.

- 1 Corinthians 10:31, NASB

"And be not drunk with wine, wherein is excess;
but be filled with the Spirit."

- Ephesians 5:18, KJV

"Whatever you do, do your work heartily,
as for the Lord rather than for men."

- Colossians 3:23, NASB

"You will have plenty to eat, until you are full, and you will praise the name of the LORD your God, who has worked wonders for you…"

- Joel 2:26, NIV

Prayers
Ascending

PRAY WITHOUT CEASING

- 1 Thessalonians 5:17, NASB

"Be anxious for nothing, but in everything by prayer and supplication with thanksgiving let your requests be made known to God."

- Philippians 4:6, NASB

I should cultivate a constant attitude of prayer:

"Let us therefore come boldly unto the throne of grace,
that we may obtain mercy, and find grace to help in time of need."

- Hebrews 4:16, KJV

God's promises regarding prayer:

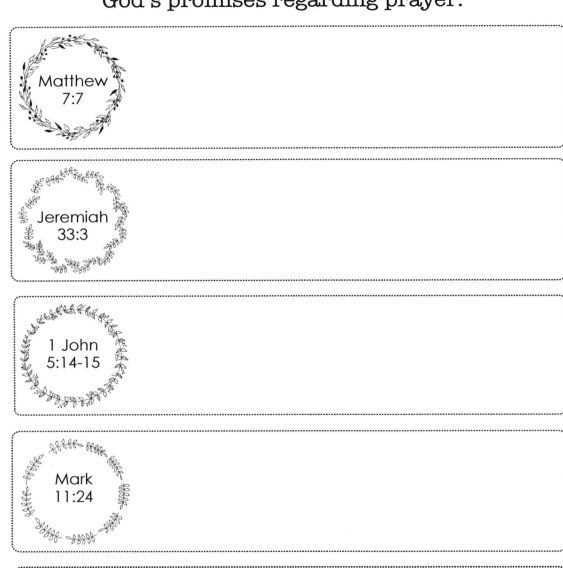

Matthew
7:7

Jeremiah
33:3

1 John
5:14-15

Mark
11:24

James
1:5

My Requests & God's Answers

"Seek the LORD while He may be found; call on Him while he is near."

- Isaiah 55:6, NIV

ASK

and it shall be given unto you,

SEEK

and ye shall find,

KNOCK

and it shall be opened unto you.

· LUKE 11:9, KJV ·

"In the same way the Spirit also helps our weakness;
for we do not know how to pray as we should, but the Spirit Himself
intercedes for us with groanings too deep for words."

- Romans 8:26, NASB

"Call upon Me in the day of trouble; I shall rescue you,
and you will honor Me."

- Psalm 50:15, NASB

PRAYING FOR YOUR HUSBAND
FROM HEAD TO TOE

http://lovinglifeathome.com

Pray for His Brain:
Ask that God would keep it sharp and focused and that his thoughts would not be conformed to this world, but would be transformed and renewed by the power of God. (Romans 12:2)

Pray for His Eyes:
Ask that he would guard them diligently and would set no worthless thing before them. (Psalm 101:3)

Pray for His Ears:
Ask that they'd be tuned to hear God's still, small voice and that your husband would always remain attentive to the Holy Spirit's promptings. (1 Thessalonians 5:19; Isaiah 30:9)

Pray for His Mouth:
Ask that no unwholesome talk would proceed from it, but only what is good for building others up. Pray that your husband would always and only speak the truth in love. (Ephesians 4:15, 29)

Pray for His Heart:
Ask that Christ would sit enthroned upon it, that your husband would love God with all his heart and soul and might, that he'd love his neighbor as himself. (Mark 12:30-31) Pray for his heart to remain soft toward you (Proverbs 5:18-19), and to be knitted to the hearts of his children. (Malachi 4:6)

Pray for His Arms:
Ask that God would strengthen them and make them firm. Pray that your husband would take delight in his labor and that God would bless the work of his hands. (Psalm 90:17, Ecclesiastes 3:22)

Pray for His Legs:
Ask that God would give him strength and stamina, that your husband might run with endurance the race that is set before him, without growing weary or fainting along the way (Hebrews 12:1; Isaiah 40:31)

Pray for His Feet:
Ask that they'd be quick to flee from temptation, to turn away from evil, and to faithfully pursue wisdom, righteousness, peace, love, and truth. (2 Timothy 2:22; Psalm 34:14; Proverbs 4:5-7)

P
Praise

R
Repent

A
Ask

Y
Yield

"But you, when you pray, go into your inner room,
close your door and pray to your Father who is in secret, and your
Father who sees what is done in secret will reward you."

- Matthew 6:6, NASB

"YOU DO NOT HAVE, BECAUSE YOU DO NOT ASK."

- James 4:2

"Call unto Me, and I will answer thee, and show thee
great and mighty things, which thou knowest not."

- Jeremiah 33:3, KJV

A Joyful Heart

Dancing for Joy

"Praise Him with timbrel and dancing;
Praise Him with stringed instruments and pipe."

- Psalm 150:4, NAB

With a Song in My Heart

"The LORD is my strength and my shield;
my heart trusts in Him, and He helps me.
My heart leaps for joy, and with my song I praise Him."

- Psalm 28:7, NIV

Where do I find joy?

"As pressure and stress
bear down on me,
I find joy in your commands.."

- Psalm 119:143, NLT

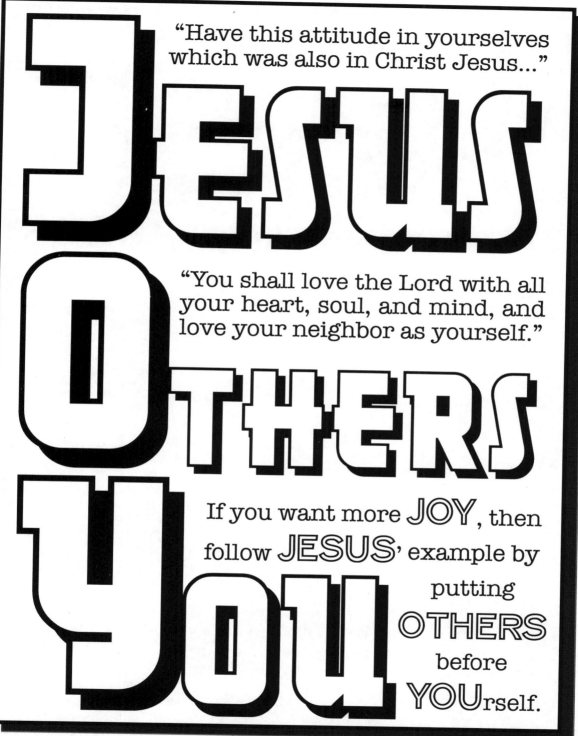

"Have this attitude in yourselves which was also in Christ Jesus..."

JESUS

"You shall love the Lord with all your heart, soul, and mind, and love your neighbor as yourself."

OTHERS

If you want more JOY, then follow JESUS' example by putting OTHERS before YOUrself.

YOU

A Merry Heart...

"Now may the God of hope fill you with all joy and peace in believing, so that you will abound in hope by the power of the Holy Spirit."

- Romans 15:13, NASB

... and a Healthy Body.

"A joyful heart is good medicine,
But a broken spirit dries up the bones."

- Proverbs 17:22, NASB

WHAT THE BIBLE

Jude 1:24

Psalm 30:5

Romans 12:15

Galatians 5:22

SAYS ABOUT JOY

Psalm 68:3

1 Thess. 5:16

3 John 1:4

Habakuk 3:18

Rejoice in the Lord always, and again I say, rejoice. - Phil. 4:4

"You have endowed him with eternal blessings and
given him the joy of your presence."

- Psalm 21:6, NLT

Rejoice always

1 Thessalonians 5:16

Even in the midst of sorrow and sadness...

"Weeping may tarry for the night, but joy comes with the morning.."

- Psalm 30:5, ESV

...I will praise the Lord and rejoice in Him.

"God gives wisdom, knowledge, and joy to those who please him."

- Ecclesiastes 2:26, NLT

"Splendor and majesty are before him;
strength and joy are in his dwelling place."

- 1 Chronicles 16:27, NIV

Giving
Thanks

I am thankful for the people
God has placed in my life...

"I thank my God
upon every remembrance of you..."

- Philippians 1:3, KJV

...and for the many gifts &
blessings He has given me.

"In every thing give thanks:
for this is the will of God
in Christ Jesus
concerning you."

- 1 Thess. 5:18, KJV

COUNT YOUR

BLESSINGS:

He provides for my needs.

"And day by day... breaking bread
in their homes, they received their food
with glad and generous hearts."

- Acts 2:46, ESV

IN
EVERYTHING
GIVE
THANKS.

- 1 Thessalonians 5:18 -

I am thankful for the love
& compassion He's shown me.

"Enter into his gates with thanksgiving,
and into his courts with praise:
be thankful unto him, and bless his name."

- Psalm 100:4, KJV

I am thankful that
He hears my prayers.

"Devote yourselves to prayer with an alert mind and a thankful heart."

- Colossians 4:2, NLT

What the Bible says about gratitude:

Ephesians
5:20

Colossians
3:15-16

1 Thessalonians
5:18

Colossians
2: 7

Philemon
1:4

"And whatever you do, whether in word or deed, do it all in the name of the Lord Jesus, giving thanks to God the Father through Him."

- Colossians 3:17, NIV

"Whatever is noble, whatever is right, whatever is pure,
whatever is lovely, whatever is admirable—
if anything is excellent or praiseworthy—think about such things."

- Philippians 4:8, NIV

Love
Abounding

He covers me with His love.

"He has brought me to his banquet hall,
& his banner over me is love."

- Song of Solomon 2:4, NASB

"Let love be without hypocrisy.
Abhor what is evil; cling to what is good."

- Romans 12:9, NASB

LISTEN

OBEY

"Whoever belongs to God
hears what God says."

- John 8:47, NIV

"If you love Me,
obey My commandments."

- John 14:15, NLT

VALUE

"The LORD values the lives
of His faithful followers."

- Psalm 116:15, NET

ENCOURAGE

"Encourage one another and
build each other up."

-1 Thessalonians 5:17, NIV

EVERLASTINGS.

The LORD appeared to us in the past, saying: 'I have loved you with an everlasting love; I have drawn you with unfailing kindness.'"

- Jeremiah 31:3, NIV

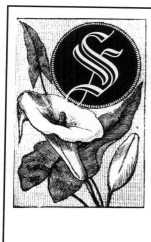

She will comfort, encourage & do him only good as long as there is life within her.

- Proverbs 31:12, AMP

O, Perfect Love,
all human thought transcending...

"There is no fear in love; but perfect love casts out fear...."

- 1 John 4:18, NASB

Our love for one another
should reflect God's love for us.

"No one has ever seen God; but if we love one another,
God lives in us and His love is made complete in us."

- 1 John 4:!2, NIV

What the Bible says about love:

1 John 4 : 20

John 13 : 34

1 Corinthians 13 : 4-8

1 Peter 3 : 8-9

Matthew 5 : 43-45

Romans 13 : 8-9

Luke 6 32-35

Jesus is our example.

"Greater love hath no man than this,
that a man lay down his life for his friends."

- John 15:13, KJV

We are to be imitators of Christ.

"Now about your love for one another
we do not need to write to you,
for you yourselves have been taught
by God to love each other."

- 1 Thessalonians 4:9, NIV

LOVE IS PATIENT, LOVE IS KIND & IS NOT JEALOUS; IT DOES NOT BRAG & IS NOT ARROGANT; IT DOES NOT ACT UNBECOMINGLY, IT DOES NOT SEEK ITS OWN, LOVE IS NOT PROVOKED & DOES NOT TAKE INTO ACCOUNT A WRONG SUFFERED; REJOICES NOT WITH UNRIGHTEOUSNESS, BUT REJOICES WITH THE TRUTH; BEARS ALL THINGS, BELIEVES ALL THINGS, HOPES ALL THINGS, ENDURES ALL THINGS, LOVE NEVER FAILS. 1 COR. 13:4-8

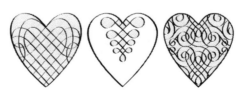

"We have come to know and have believed the love which
God has for us. God is love, and the one who abides in love
abides in God, and God abides in him."

- 1 John 4:16, NASB

Cultivating
Oneness

Making Beautiful
Music Together

"Sing to the LORD with grateful praise;
make music to our God on the harp."

- Psalm 147:7, NIV

Many waters cannot quench love; rivers cannot sweep it away.

- Song of Solomon 8:7
NIV

Hugs & Kisses

"Let him kiss me
with the kisses of his mouth—for your
love is more delightful than wine."

- Song of Solomon 1:1, NIV

Evening Strolls

"Awake, north wind, and come, south wind!
Blow on my garden, that its fragrance may spread everywhere.
Let my beloved come into his garden and taste its choice fruits."

- Song of Solomon 3:4, NIV

"Drink your fill of Love."

- Song of Solomon 5:1
NIV

"I found the one my heart loves.
I held him and would not let him go...."

- Song of Solomon 3:4, NIV

Happy Companionship

"...I am faint with love.
His left arm is under my head,
and his right arm embraces me."

- Song of Solomon 2:5-6, NIV

Sweet Intimacy

"My beloved is to me
a sachet of myrrh
resting between my breasts."

- Song of Solomon 1:13, NIV

My body belongs to my husband...

"...Rejoice in the wife of your youth. As a loving hind
and a graceful doe, Let her breasts satisfy you at all times;
be exhilarated always with her love."

- Proverbs 5:18-19, NASB

...and his belongs to me.

"The wife does not have authority over her own body,
but the husband does; and likewise also the husband does not have
authority over his own body, but the wife does."

- 1 Corinthians 7:4, NASB

"Therefore a man shall leave his father and mother and hold fast to his wife, and the two shall become one flesh."

- Ephesians 5:31, ESV

Growing Together

"Teach us to number our days,
That we may present to You
a heart of wisdom."

- Psalm 90:12, NASB

"When times are good, be happy;
but when times are bad, consider this:
God has made the one as well
as the other..."

- Ecclesiastes 7:14, NIV

"And he shall be like a tree
planted by the rivers of water,
that bringeth forth his fruit in his season;
his leaf also shall not wither;
and whatsoever he doeth shall prosper."

- Psalm 1:3, KJV

YOUR WIFE SHALL BE LIKE A FRUITFUL VINE WITHIN YOUR HOUSE, YOUR CHILDREN LIKE OLIVE PLANTS AROUND YOUR TABLE.

{ Psalm 128:3 NASB }

I must examine myself ...

"Examine yourselves to see whether you are in the faith;
test yourselves. Do you not realize that Christ Jesus is in you—
unless, of course, you fail the test?"

- 2 Corinthians 13:5, NIV

... and take every thought captive.

"We are destroying speculations and every lofty thing
raised up against the knowledge of God, and we are taking
every thought captive to the obedience of Christ."

- 2 Corinthians 10:5, NASB

Be kind to one another, tender-hearted, forgiving each other...

- Ephesians 4:32, NASB

Love One Another

"A new command I give you: Love one another.
As I have loved you, so you must love one another."

- John 13:34, NASB

There's no coasting in marriage.

"... live a life worthy of the Lord and please Him in every way:
bearing fruit in every good work, growing in the knowledge of God."

- Colossians 1:10, NIV

Love serves love.

"Therefore encourage one another and build each other up,
just as in fact you are doing."

- 1 Thessalonians 5:11, NIV

Lifelong Friendship

"Oil and perfume make the heart glad,
so a man's counsel is sweet to his friend."

- Proverbs 27:9, NASB

"An excellent
wife is the crown
of her husband,
but she who
shames him
is like rottenness
in his bones."

- Proverbs 12:4 -

"Let us think of ways to motivate one another
to acts of love and good works."

- Hebrews 10:24, NLT

Check your answers:

Qualities of a Virtuous Wife

(solutions to puzzle on page 107)

```
J O Y F U L A Y H T R O W T S U R T P U B
M U P R A I S E D I D C D U M R A N O M L
T Y E C N A S C T S E N O H A Y E E D L E
R D S A K I N D N T R I O M A M N E W R S
Y E T P W R T C A E C E G C F C V F O E S
I I V A L U A B L E S V D H U O J O R A E
G F I B R I L R R F I L I L N R R S B D
N I R L H E S P E D A T T T U S E T H L E
I N T E L L I G E N T A N R F C N U I E S
K G U S A H A N O F R E E B I I A N P N S
R I O T P P Y B D R D R R I A E L A F C G
O D U E P T L I S U Q C E G F N A T U O N
W W S A R E H E R I S N V T O T U E L U I
D A K D E Y D P M T I T E O R I T N N R F
R L E F C L I N A F V O R W S O I D S A R
A H T A I G A W G U E F L I T U R I Y G O
H N O S A N R H O L H T U L O S I N A I M
E T I T T U F O D R I S F L A U P M W N T
C O N U E T A S L U F L L I K S S U R G E
L E S N D F N T Y P P A H N Z I U Q D I L
G E N E R O U S E M X I T G N O R T S O F
```

More Books to Help You
Build a Better Marriage

25 Ways to Communicate Respect to Your Husband: A Handbook for Wives

We get out of marriage what we put into it. If you'd like for your husband to be more attentive, to notice and admire you, to spend more time with you, and to be respectful of your wishes and opinions, then you must treat him as you want to be treated. This book outlines twenty-five tried-and-true ways to do exactly that, with practical suggestions at the end of each chapter for putting the principles into practice.

25 Ways to Show Love to Your Wife: A Handbook for Husbands

In this companion volume to *25 Ways to Communicate Respect,* author Doug Flanders shares twenty-five tips for husbands who want to improve their marriage. Side effects from implementing the principles set forth in these pages may include a stronger marriage, a happier home, a more satisfying sex life, improved communication skills, a deeper love for your spouse, and greater respect from her in return.

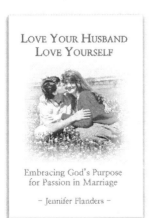

Love Your Husband/Love Yourself: Embracing God's Purpose for Passion in Marriage

"This book is the talk your mother never had the nerve to have with you." Packed with loads of Biblical wisdom, scientific studies, and humorous anecdotes, *Love Your Husband/ Love Yourself* is a must read for every married woman. It will help you unlock the secret to a happy, healthy, loving, lifelong relationship with your spouse.

One Last Word from the Author:

I hope you've enjoyed working your way through this book as much as I enjoyed creating it. I pray that by meditating upon God's word and on His purpose for marriage, as well as your husband's most admirable qualities and the sweet memories you share, you have seen both relationships grow deeper and more joyous.

For more marriage encouragement, please check out the titles on the opposite page, follow my blog (*http://lovinglifeathome.com*), or join me on Facebook (*https://www.facebook.com/love.your.husband.yourself*).

If you have any questions or suggestions, I would love to hear from you! You may write *flandersfamily@flandersfamily.info* or contact me through my family's website (*http://www.flandersfamily.info*). Although I read every message I receive, time constraints unfortunately do not allow me to respond personally to most of them.

Other books in this series:

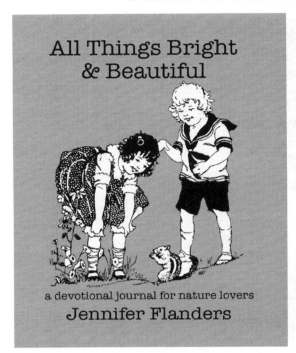

All Things Bright
& Beautiful

a devotional journal for nature lovers
Jennifer Flanders

Be Still, My Soul

a devotional journal for boys
Jennifer Flanders

Bread of Heaven

a devotional journal for culinary artists
Jennifer Flanders

Moment by Moment

a devotional journal for girls
Jennifer Flanders

"Your relationship to your husband may be the only marriage book your children ever read. What lessons will they take with them when they leave home?"

- Jennifer Flanders

Loving Life at Home

46794804R00121

Made in the USA
Charleston, SC
25 September 2015